The

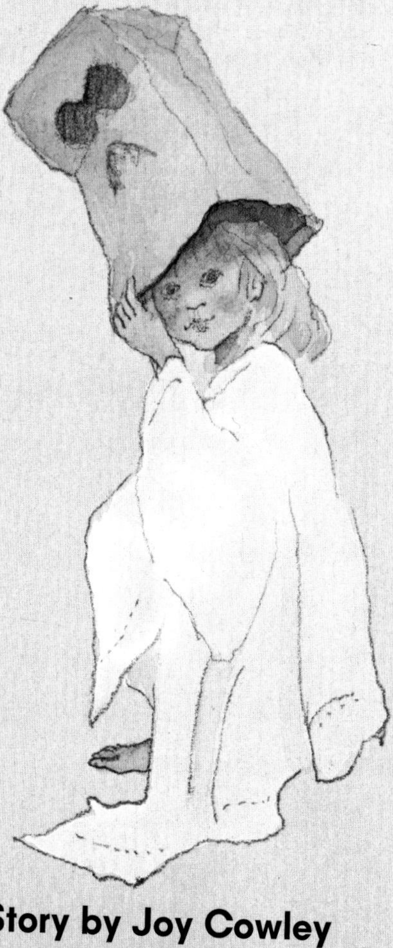

Story by Joy Cowley
Illustrations by Robyn Belton

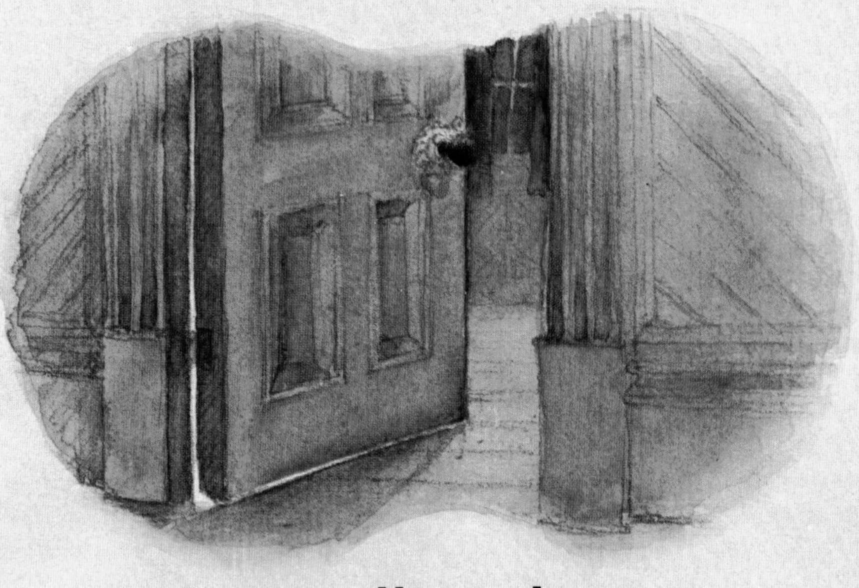

I see the door.

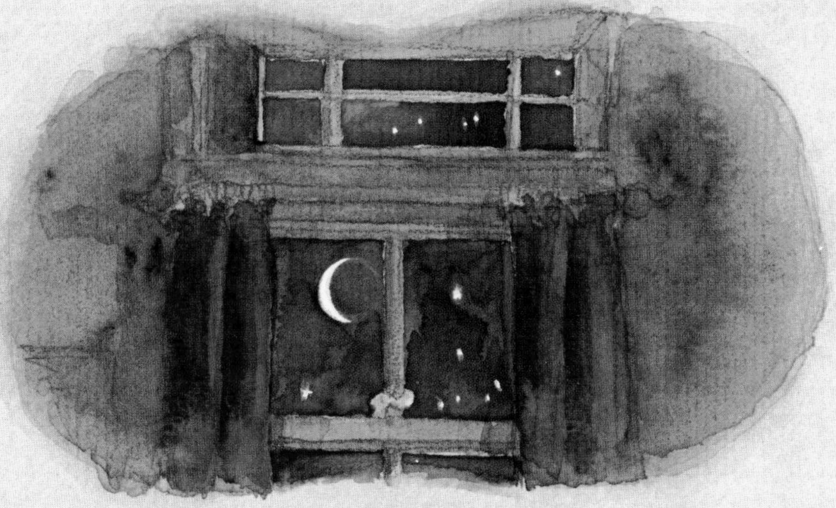

I see the window.

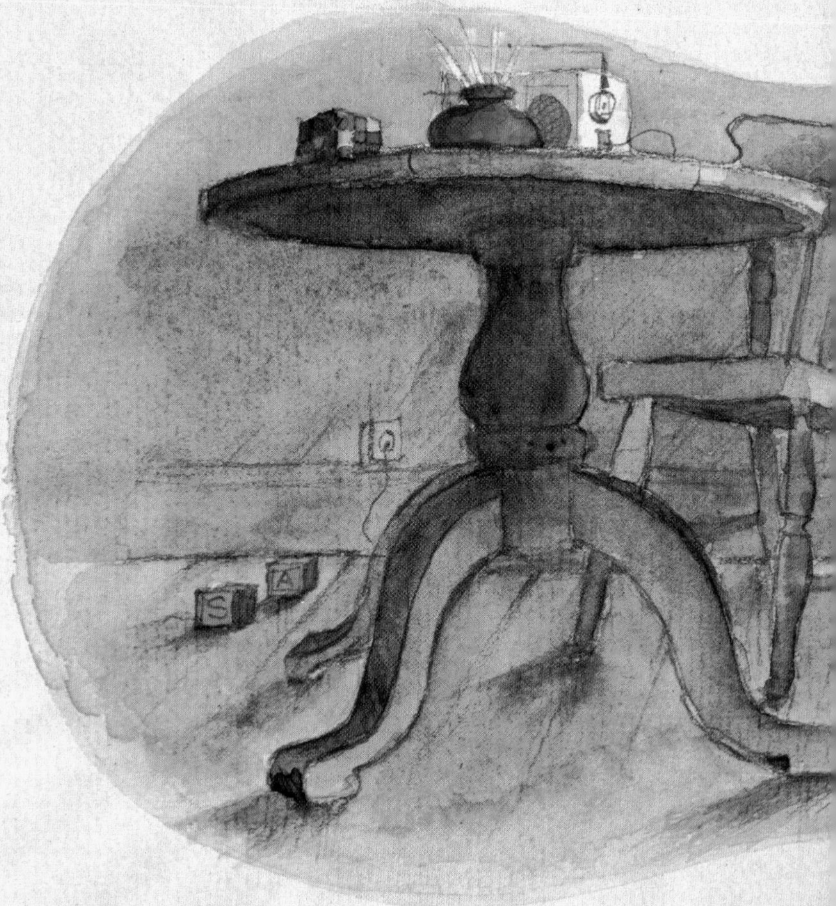

I see the table.

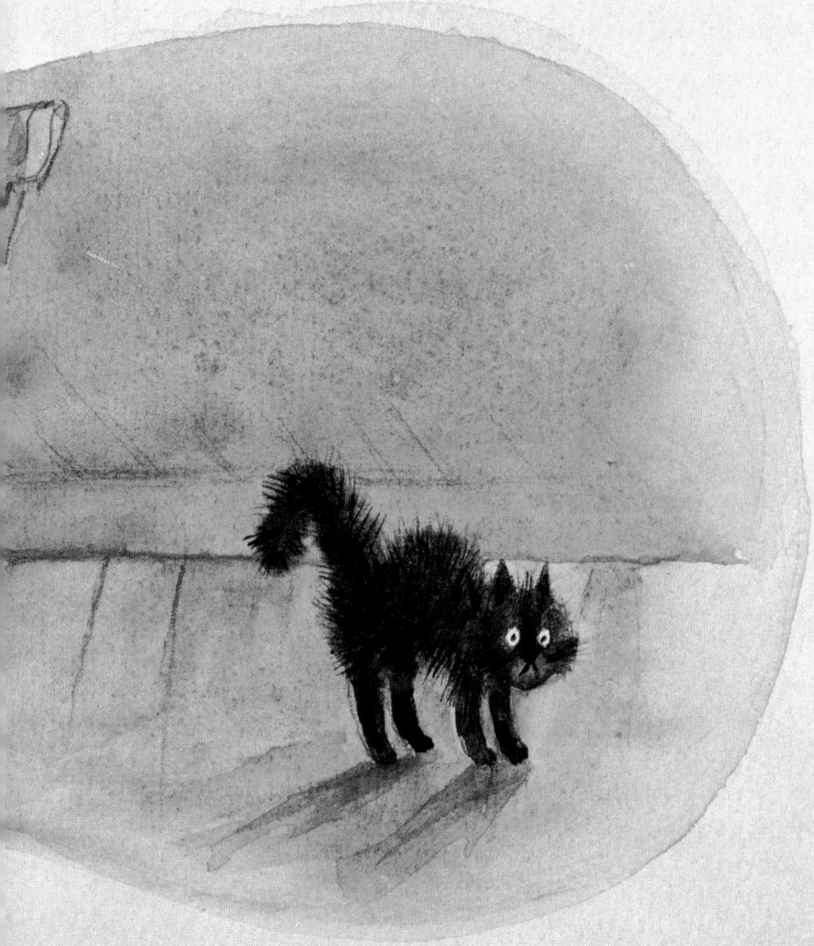

I see the cat.

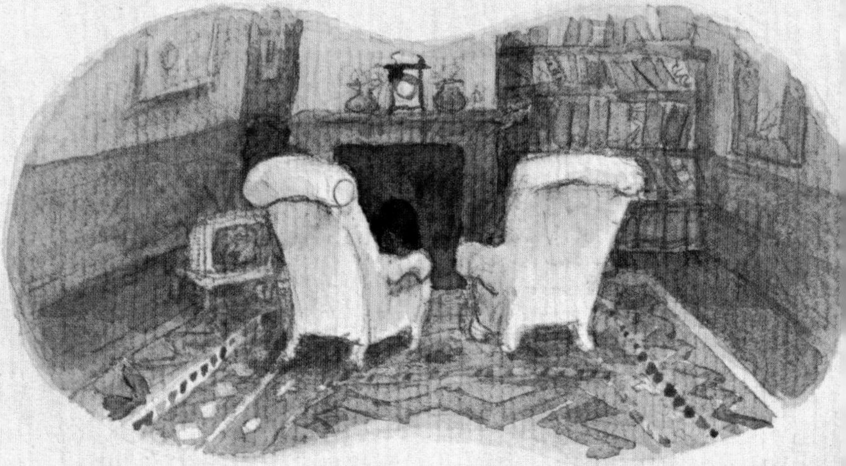

I see the chairs.

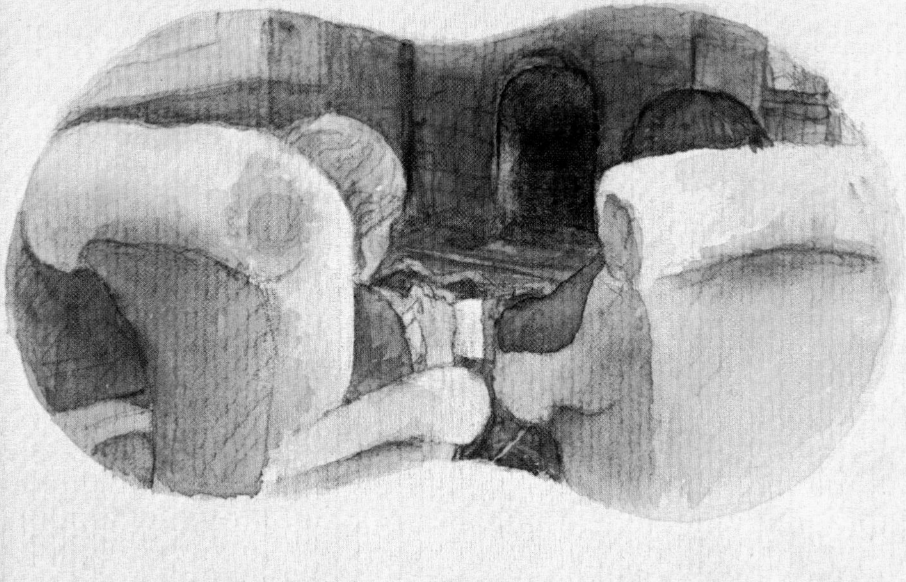

I see Mom and Dad.

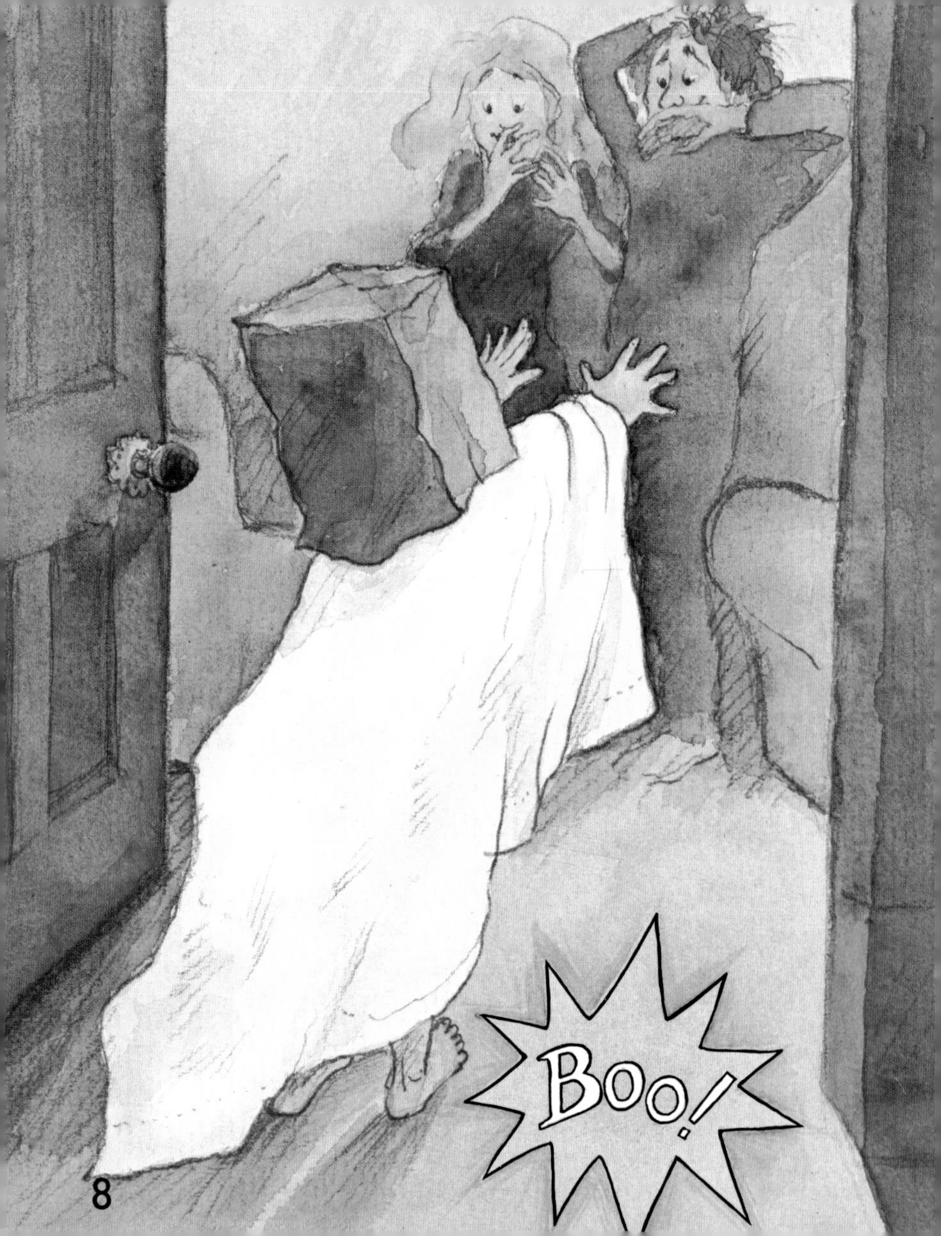
Boo!